3-

D1039883

ICONS

SWEDEN STYLE

SWEDEN

Exteriors Interiors

STYLE
Details

EDITOR **Angelika Taschen**

TASCHEN

HONG KONG KÖLN LONDON LOS ANGELES MADRID PARIS TOKYO

Front cover: Well-cushioned: a rural style living room.
Couverture: *Coussins confortables pour le dos : dans un salon d'inspiration campagnarde.*
Umschlagvorderseite: Weiche Kissen im Rücken: In einem ländlich inspirierten Wohnzimmer.

Back cover: Aromatic camomile: in Groddagården House on Gotland.
Dos de couverture: *Le parfum de la camomille : dans la maison Groddagården sur l'île de Gotland.*
Umschlagrückseite: Der Duft von Kamille: Im Haus Groddagården auf Gotland.

To stay informed about upcoming TASCHEN titles, please request our magazine at www.taschen.com/magazine or write to TASCHEN, Hohenzollernring 53, D-50672 Cologne, Germany, contact@taschen.com, Fax: +49-221-254919. We will be happy to send you a free copy of our magazine which is filled with information about all of our books.

© 2005 TASCHEN GmbH
Hohenzollernring 53, D-50672 Köln
www.taschen.com

Edited by Angelika Taschen, Berlin
Layout and general project management by Stephanie Bischoff, Cologne
Texts by Christiane Reiter, Berlin
Lithography by Horst Neuzner, Cologne
English translation by Pauline Cumbers, Frankfurt am Main
French translation by Anne Charrière, Croissy/Seine

Printed in Italy
ISBN 978-3-8228-4016-0

CONTENTS SOMMAIRE INHALT

A country as pretty as a picture – in the truest sense of the term. When you think of Sweden you see Pippi Longstocking charging through Villa Villekulla, Ronja the Robber's Daughter wandering through Matti Wood and Michel from Loenneberga stuck in the soup tureen. You dream of being on a bench in front of a holiday home on Saltkrokan with a view of the Schären from lattice windows, or in a kitchen in Bullerby, where colourful rag rugs muffle the creaking of the floorboards and a metal stove roars. Swedish authors, first and foremost Astrid Lindgren, introduced a wonderland into our dreams for which we still long and which still causes us to marvel. For often Sweden is in fact quite inaccessible – with its different climate zones, its forests extending beyond the horizon, and its coasts teeming with islands. The almost 450,000 square kilometres are inhabited by just nine million people, and they have adapted perfectly to the harshness of

SWEDEN FROM ITS PRETTIEST SIDES

Christiane Reiter

C'est un pays tout droit sorti des livres d'images – au sens propre : quand on pense à la Suède, n'aperçoit-on pas Fifi Brindacier filer à travers la villa Villekulla, Ronja, fille de brigand, parcourir la forêt de Mattis, et Michel de Lönneberga caché dans la soupière? Ne se voit-on pas en rêve à Saltkrokan sur le banc de la maison de campagne dont les fenêtres à croisillons donnent sur des récifs, ou dans la cuisine du village de Bou-can, où ronfle un poêle en fer et où des tapis aux patchworks multicolores étouffent les craquements du plancher ? Les écri-vains suédois, et Astrid Lindgren la première, ont introduit dans nos chambres d'enfants un monde merveilleux qui éveille notre étonnement et notre nostalgie. Car en fait, la Suède n'est pas toujours si facile d'accès, avec ses zones climatiques très contrastées, ses forêts à perte de vue, et ses rives d'îles innom-brables. Sur à peine 450 000 kilomètres carrés ne vivent aujourd'hui que neuf millions d'habitants, mais ils se sont parfai-tement installés dans cette rude contrée. En Suède, la maison

Es ist ein Land wie aus dem Bilderbuch – und das im wahrsten Sinne des Wortes: Wer an Schweden denkt, sieht Pippi Langstrumpf durch die Villa Kunterbunt sausen, Ronja Räubertochter durch den Mattiswald streifen und Michel von Lönneberga in der Suppenschüssel stecken. Er träumt sich auf die Bank vor dem Ferienhaus auf Saltkrokan, das aus Sprossenfenstern über die Schären blickt, oder in die Küche von Bullerbü, in der bunte Flickenteppiche das Knarzen der Dielen dämpfen und ein Eisenherd bullert. Schwedische Autoren, allen voran Astrid Lindgren, haben uns eine Wunderwelt ins Kinderzimmer gebracht, nach der wir uns seither immer wieder sehnen und über die wir immer wieder staunen. Denn eigentlich ist Schweden eine oft unzugängliche Umgebung – mit den unterschiedlichsten Klimazonen, Wäldern bis hinter den Horizont und Küsten voller ungezählter Inseln. Auf knapp 450.000 Quadratkilometern leben nur neun Millionen Menschen – doch sie haben sich in dieser rauen Region perfekt eingerichtet. In

the region. In Sweden, the focal point of people's lives since time immemorial has been their own four walls, offering protection from nature, while at the same time making the best of it. Where else does the sun shine so brightly on painted yellow walls, do the colours of the flowers on cushions and covers glow so radiantly, do the herbs in stoneware pots smell so aromatically? Many of the furnishings and accessories are made of natural materials and succeed in being both useful and decorative. In Sweden, "design" does not designate elitist luxury, but is there for everyone and is an important component of everyday life. Be it in a wind-swept fisherman's hut on Gotland, a city apartment above the roofs of Stockholm, or a castle in Uppland revelling in Gustavian elegance: the style of Sweden creates a particular kind of hospitality and cosiness – like in a picture book.

est le refuge et le centre de la vie familiale. Elle protège de la nature environnante, et en tire ce qu'elle a de meilleur. Existe-t-il un autre pays où le soleil brille aussi joliment sur des murs peints en jaune, où les couleurs des fleurs paraissent aussi lumineuses sur les coussins et les couvertures, où les herbes dégagent un tel arôme dans leurs pots en grès ? Beaucoup de meubles et d'accessoires sont en matériaux naturels et la prouesse est d'en avoir fait des objets à la fois d'usage courant et de décoration. Le «design» n'est pas en Suède un luxe élitaire, mais un bien commun, un ingrédient important du quotidien. Que ce soit dans la cabane de pêcheur exposée à tous les vents sur l'île de Gotland, dans un appartement qui donne sur les toits de Stockholm ou un château d'Uppland, baignant dans l'élégance gustavienne : le style suédois crée un art très particulier de l'hospitalité et du bien-être – comme dans un livre d'images.

Schweden sind die eigenen vier Wände seit jeher der Lebensmittelpunkt jeder Familie, sie bieten Schutz vor der umliegenden Natur und holen zugleich das Beste aus ihr heraus. Wo sonst leuchtet die Sonne so schön auf gelb gestrichenen Wänden, finden sich die Farben der Blumen so strahlend auf Kissen oder Decken wieder und duften die Kräuter in den Steinguttöpfen so aromatisch wie hier? Auch viele Möbel und Accessoires greifen natürliche Materialien auf und bringen das Kunststück fertig, Gebrauchsgegenstand und Schmuckstück in einem zu sein. „Design" bezeichnet in Schweden keinen elitären Luxus, sondern ist für alle da und wichtiger Bestandteil des Alltags. Ganz egal, ob in einer windschiefen Fischerhütte auf Gotland, einer Stadtwohnung über den Dächern von Stockholm oder einem Schloss in Uppland, das in gustavianischer Eleganz schwelgt: Schwedischer Stil schafft eine ganz besondere Art von Gastfreundschaft und Gemütlichkeit – eben wie im Bilderbuch.

"…Katharina did a detour via the veranda, stopping there to observe how the wide river outside changed its colour from the brightest of blue to ultramarine, violet and, along the banks, a golden green…"

Marianne Fredriksson, in: *Älskade barn*

«…Katharina fit le détour par la véranda, s'y arrêta et observa les changements de teinte du large fleuve : du bleu le plus clair, il passait à l'outremer, au lilas et le long des berges au vert doré…»

Marianne Fredriksson, dans: *Älskade barn*

»…Katharina nahm den Umweg über die Veranda, blieb dort stehen und beobachtete, wie draußen der breite Strom seine Farbe vom hellsten Blau ins Ultramarin, zu Lila und an den Ufern entlang zu goldenem Grün wechselte…«

Marianne Fredriksson, in: *Geliebte Tochter*

EXTERIORS

Extérieurs Aussichten

10/11 Icy nights: in front of the Ice Hotel in Jukkasjärvi, northern Sweden. *Nuits glacées : devant l'hôtel de glace à Jukkasjärvi, Suède du Nord.* Eisige Nächte: Vor dem Icehotel in Jukkasjärvi, Nordschweden.

12/13 Panorama above the water: an angular seat in front of Varpet House, near Stockholm. *Vue panoramique sur l'eau : coin assis devant la maison Varpet, près de Stockholm.* Panoramablick übers Wasser: Sitzecke vor dem Haus Varpet, bei Stockholm.

14/15 Under pointed gables: on the estate of the artist Anders Zorn, Dalarna. *Sous des pignons en pointe : dans la propriété du peintre Anders Zorn, Dalarna.* Unter spitzen Giebeln: Auf dem Anwesen des Malers Anders Zorn, Dalarna.

16/17 All in green: garden of the naturalist Carl von Linné, Uppland. *Tout en vert : dans le jardin du naturaliste Carl von Linné, Uppland.* Ganz in Grün: Im Garten des Naturforschers Carl von Linné, Uppland.

18/19 Brilliant red: a lonely wooden house in a forest. *Rouge lumineux : maison en bois le long d'un chemin forestier à l'écart du monde.* Leuchtend rot: Ein Holzhaus an einem einsamen Waldweg.

20/21 One of Sweden's famous addresses: Astrid Lindgren's birthplace, in Näs. *L'une des adresses célèbres de Suède : la maison où est née d'Astrid Lindgren, Näs.* Eine berühmte Adresse Schwedens: Das Geburtshaus von Astrid Lindgren in Näs.

22/23 A leafy roof: the home of the draughtsman Albert Engström, Uppland. *Sous un toit de feuilles : la maison du dessinateur Albert Engström, Uppland.* Unter einem Blätterdach: Das Haus des Zeichners Albert Engström, Uppland.

24/25 Reflections in the water: the farmhouse owned by the illustrator Carl Larsson, Dalarna. *Reflets dans l'eau : devant la cour de l'illustrateur Carl Larsson, Dalarna.* Im Wasser gespiegelt: Vor dem Hof des Illustrators Carl Larsson, Dalarna.

26/27 Radiantly white window frames: the house of Carl von Linné in Hammarby, Uppland. *Cadres de fenêtre d'un blanc éclatant : chez Carl von Linné à Hammarby, Uppland.* Strahlend weiße Fensterrahmen: Bei Carl von Linné in Hammarby, Uppland.

28/29 A grassy roof: the former Kyrkhult farmhouse, today part of an open-air museum. *Toit de chaume : l'ancienne ferme de Kyrkhult, aujourd'hui au musée de plein air.* Ein Dach aus Gras: Der ehemalige Bauernhof von Kyrkhult, heute im Freilichtmuseum.

30/31 Homage to France: the classically elegant facade of Svartsjö Castle, Mälaren. *Hommage à la France : l'élégante façade classique du château de Svartsjö, Mälaren.* Hommage an Frankreich: Die klassisch-elegante Fassade von Schloss Svartsjö, Mälaren.

32/33 19th century: the romantic pavilion of Almare Stäket. *XIXᵉ siècle : le romantique pavillon lacustre d'Almare Stäket.* Aus dem 19. Jahrhundert: Der romantische Seepavillon von Almare Stäket.

34/35 Model for Villa Villekulla: the "Yellow House" was built by Astrid Lindgren's father. *Modèle pour la Villa Villekulla : la «maison jaune» a été bâtie par le père d'Astrid Lindgren.* Vorbild für die Villa Kunterbunt: Das »Gelbe Haus« baute Astrid Lindgrens Vater.

36/37 A sunny spot: in front of the angler's house in Varpet in southeast Stockholm. *Pour les heures ensoleillées : devant la petite maison de pêche de Varpet, au sud-est de Stockholm.* Für Sonnenstunden: Vor dem Angelhäuschen von Varpet im Südosten Stockholms.

38/39 Pretty as a picture: the lovingly refurbished turn-of-the-century Varpet House. *Comme dans un livre d'images : la maison Varpet, restaurée avec amour, date du tournant du siècle.* Wie aus dem Bilderbuch: Das liebevoll restaurierte Jahrhundertwendehaus Varpet.

40/41 Inspired by the sea: studio of the draughtsman Albert Engström on Väddö, Uppland. *Inspiration au bord de la mer : l'atelier du dessinateur Albert Engström à Väddö, Uppland.* Inspiration am Meer: Das Atelier des Zeichners Albert Engström auf Väddö, Uppland.

42/43 Wind-swept: Johan Brauner's house on Gotland, 90 km from the coast of Sweden. *Battue par les vents : la maison de Johan Brauner l'île de Gotland, à 90 km de la côte suédoise.* Windschief: Bei Johan Brauner auf Gotland, 90 km vor der schwedischen Küste.

44/45 A gift: King Oskar I had this wooden villa in Uppland built for his mistress. *Cadeau : cette villa en bois d'Uppland a été construite par le roi Oskar Ier pour sa maîtresse.* Das Geschenk: Die Holzvilla in Uppland ließ König Oskar I. für seine Maitresse bauen.

46/47 A place in the sun: today the house of designer Carl Malmsten is a museum. *Une place au soleil : aujourd'hui, la maison du designer Carl Malmsten est un musée.* Ein Platz an der Sonne: Heute ist das Haus des Designers Carl Malmsten ein Museum.

48/49 Like a fortress: the former farmhouse and inn Groddagården in the north of Gotland. *Comme une forteresse : l'ancienne ferme et auberge Groddagården au nord de Gotland.* Wie eine Festung: Das ehemalige Bauern- und Wirtshaus Groddagården im Norden Gotlands.

"...On the floor were brand new colourful rag rugs. The metal rods on the cooker were wrapped in red, green, and white crepe paper..."

Astrid Lindgren, in: *The Children of Noisy Village*

«...Le sol était couvert de tapis en patchworks, multicolores tout neufs. Les barres en fer du four étaient enveloppées de papier crépon rouge, vert et blanc...»

Astrid Lindgren, dans : *Nous, les enfants du village Bouca*

»...Auf dem Fußboden lagen ganz neue bunte Flickenteppiche. Die Eisenstangen am Herd waren mit rotem, grünem und weißem Krepppapier umwickelt...«

Astrid Lindgren, in: *Die Kinder aus Bullerbü*

INTERIORS

Intérieurs Einsichten

54/55 Drinks on the rocks: at the bar of the Ice Hotel in Jukkasjärvi, northern Sweden. *On the rocks : au bar de l'hôtel de glace de Jukkasjärvi, Suède du Nord.* Drinks on the rocks: An der Bar des Icehotels in Jukkasjärvi, Nordschweden.

56/57 On ice: in the Ice Hotel guests sleep on warm hides. *Etendues sur la glace : dans l'hôtel de glace, on dort sur des fourrures chauffantes.* Auf Eis gelegt: Im Icehotel schläft man auf wärmenden Fellen.

58/59 Well-cushioned: a rural style living-room. *Coussins confortables pour le dos : dans un salon d'inspiration campagnarde.* Weiche Kissen im Rücken: In einem ländlich inspirierten Wohnzimmer.

60/61 Highly decorative: an iron stove beside a huge wooden chest. *Richement décorés : cheminée de fer et coffre en bois imposant.* Reich verziert: Ein eiserner Kamin neben einer mächtigen Holztruhe.

62/63 A reddish hue: Carl Larsson designed the lampshades for his dining room himself. *Lueur rougeoyante : Carl Larsson a lui-même dessiné les abat-jour de sa salle à manger.* Rötlicher Schein: Die Lampenschirme für sein Esszimmer entwarf Carl Larsson selbst.

64/65 Pride of place: Karin Larsson installed her loom in the house in Dalarna. *Bijou : dans sa maison de Dalarna, Karin Larsson a aussi installé son métier à tisser.* Schmuckstück: Im Haus in Dalarna stellte Karin Larsson auch ihren Webstuhl auf.

66/67 "The rose of love": the name of the woven curtain in Karin Larsson's room. *« La rose d'amour » : c'est le nom que Karin Larsson a donné au rideau tissé main de sa chambre.* »Die Liebesrose«: So nannte Karin Larsson den gewebten Vorhang zu ihrem Zimmer.

68/69 White and blue: for Carl Larsson the sitting room was also his "Temple to Lethargy". *Salon en blanc et bleu : pour Carl Larsson, le salon état aussi le « Temple de la paresse ».* Wohnraum in Weiß und Blau: Für Carl Larsson war der Salon auch der »Tempel der Faulheit«.

70/71 A little severe: the anteroom of the Hazeliushuset in the open-air museum. *Un soupçon de sévérité : l'antichambre de la Hazeliushuset au musée de plein air.* Ein Hauch von Strenge: Das Vorzimmer des Hazeliushuset im Freilichtmuseum.

72/73 Velvet and silk: in the elegantly opulent salon of Villa Zorngården, Dalarna. *Velours et soie : dans l'élégant et fastueux salon de la villa Zorngården, Dalarna.* Samt und Seide: Im üppig-eleganten Salon der Villa Zorngården, Dalarna.

74/75 Seventh heaven: the Gustavian guest-room in Zorngården, Dalarna. *Dormir au septième ciel : chambre d'hôtes à Zorngården, Dalarna.* Himmlisch schlafen: Das gustavianische Gästezimmer von Zorngården, Dalarna.

76/77 Like in Paris: the splendid anteroom of Leufsta Castle, Uppland. *Comme à Paris : la somptueuse antichambre du château de Leufsta, Uppland.* Wie in Paris: Das prachtvolle Vorzimmer von Schloss Leufsta, Uppland.

78/79 Cooking in copper: the kitchen in Leufsta Castle, Uppland. *Une vaisselle de cuivre : dans la cuisine du château de Leufsta, Uppland.* Kochen mit Kupfergeschirr: In der Küche von Schloss Leufsta, Uppland.

80/81 Source of warmth: the tiled stove in Madame's room in Zorngården, Dalarna. *Source de chaleur : le poêle de faïence de Zorngården, Dalarna.* Wärmequelle: Der Kachelofen im Zimmer der Hausherrin von Zorngården, Dalarna.

82/83 Sparse ambience: a simple bedroom in Groddagården on Gotland. *Atmosphère dépouillée : sobriété de la chambre à coucher de Groddagården, sur l'île de Gotland.* Karge Atmosphäre: Schlichtes Schlafzimmer in Groddagården auf Gotland.

84/85 The round table: in the country residence in Löfstad, Östergötland. *La table ronde : dans le château de plaisance de Löfstad, Östergötland.* Am runden Tisch: Im Landschloss von Löfstad, Östergötland.

86/87 Patterned: the fireplace in the country residence in Löfstad, Östergötland. *Mélange de motifs : devant la cheminée du château de plaisance de Löfstad, Östergötland.* Mustermix: Am Kamin des Landschlosses von Löfstad, Östergötland.

88/89 A crackling fire: today Goddagården, on Gotland, is a local heritage museum. *Près du feu crépitant : Goddagården sur l'île de Gotland est aujourd'hui un musée local.* Am lodernden Feuer: Goddagården auf Gotland ist heute ein Heimatmuseum.

90/91 Like a studio: in memory of the architect Carl Hårleman in Svartsjö Castle, Mälaren. *Comme à l'atelier : souvenirs de l'architecte Carl Hårleman au château de Svartsjö, Mälaren.* Wie im Atelier: Erinnerung an den Architekten Carl Hårleman auf Schloss Svartsjö, Mälaren.

92/93 Fine muslin: a bedroom at the Skogaholm manor house, Stockholm. *Délicate mousseline : chambre à coucher de la maison d'habitation de Skogaholmu, Stockholm.* Zartes Musselin: Ein Schlafzimmer im Gutshaus Skogaholm, Stockholm.

94/95 Supervised by Frederik I: the entrance hall of Svartsjö Castle, Mälaren. *Sous les yeux de Frédéric Ier : le hall d'entrée du château de Svartsjö, Mälaren.* Unter den Augen Frederiks I.: Die Eingangshalle von Schloss Svartsjö, Mälaren.

96/97 Floral decor: a bedroom at Svartsjö Castle, Mälaren. *Exemplaire : chambre à coucher au décor floral, château de Svartsjö, Mälaren.* Mustergültig: Ein blumig dekoriertes Schlafzimmer auf Schloss Svartsjö, Mälaren.

98/99 A creative mind: in the office of the designer Carl Malmsten in Malmstenhuset, Uppland. *Un esprit créatif : dans le bureau du designer Carl Malmsten à Malmstenhuset, Uppland.* Ein kreativer Kopf: Im Büro des Designers Carl Malmsten im Malmstenhuset, Uppland.

100/101 A soothing blue: the bedroom of antique dealer Hans Malmborg, Skåne. *Bleu apaisant : la chambre à coucher du vendeur d'antiquités Hans Malmborg, Skåne.* Beruhigend blau: Das Schlafzimmer des Antiquitätenhändlers Hans Malmborg, Skåne.

102/103 White stairway: in the apartment of Martine Colliander, Stockholm. *Marches en pierre blanche : Dans l'appartement de Martine Colliander, Stockholm.* Weiße Steinstufen: In der Wohnung von Martine Colliander, Stockholm.

104/105 A wall full of books: Martine Colliander takes the flair of the country to town. *Des livres jusqu'au plafond : Martine Colliander apporte un air de campagne à la ville.* Bücher bis unter die Decke: Martine Colliander holt Landhausflair in die Stadt.

106/107 A favourite place: Martine Colliander's kitchen. *Endroit préféré pour des mets de choix : la cuisine de Martine Colliander.* Lieblingsplatz für Lieblingsgerichte: Die Küche von Martine Colliander.

108/109 Pretty in pink: Martine Colliander's colourful bedroom. *Joli en rose : tache de couleur dans la chambre à coucher de Martine Colliander.* Pretty in pink: Farbtupfer im Schlafzimmer von Martine Colliander.

110/111 Positively yellow: the living room in Varpet in the style of the 1910s. *Accents jaunes : le salon de Varpet, dans le style des années 1910.* Gelbe Akzente: Das Wohnzimmer von Varpet im Stil der 1910er-Jahre.

112/113 The very heart of the house: the living room of Hans Malmborg and his wife Ditte in Skåne. *Trésor de la maison : le salon de Hans Malmborg et de sa femme Ditte, à Skåne.* Herzstück des Hauses: Das Wohnzimmer von Hans Malmborg und seiner Frau Ditte in Skåne.

114/115 Antique furniture: 19th - century table and chairs – at Hans Malmborg's home in Skåne. *Mobilier ancien : tables et chaises du XIXe siècle – chez Hans Malmborg à Skåne.* Antikes Mobiliar: Tisch und Stühle aus dem 19. Jahrhundert – bei Hans Malmborg in Skåne.

116/117 Unimpeded view: from the home of Johan Brauner on Gotland. *Vue imprenable : dans la maison de Johan Brauner sur l'île de Gotland.* Unversteller Blick nach draußen: Im Haus von Johan Brauner auf Gotland.

118/119 Like in the olden days: bedroom in the lovingly renovated hostel in Wreta. *Dormir comme au temps jadis : à l'auberge Wreta, rénovée avec tendresse.* Schlafen wie anno dazumal: In der liebevoll renovierten Herberge Wreta.

120/121 Sunshine and candlelight: Johan Brauner lives without electricity. *Vivre à la lumière du soleil et des bougies : Johan Brauner n'a pas besoin d'électricité.* Wohnen im Sonnen- und Kerzenlicht: Johan Brauner lebt ohne elektrischen Strom.

122/123 Just right for a nap: at Johan Brauner's home on Gotland. *Le plus bel endroit pour une sieste : chez Johan Brauner sur l'île de Gotland.* Der schönste Platz für einen Mittagsschlaf: Bei Johan Brauner auf Gotland.

124/125 Symmetry: the Kyrkhultsstugan farmhouse in the open-air museum, Stockholm. *Symétrie : à la ferme Kyrkhultsstugan du musée de plein air, Stockholm.* Symmetrie: Im Bauernhof Kyrkhultsstugan im Freilichtmuseum, Stockholm.

126/127 Light and shade: an open fire in the Kyrkhultsstugan farmhouse. *Ombres et lumière : cheminée ouverte dans la ferme de Kyrkhultsstugan.* Licht und Schatten: Offener Kamin im Bauernhof Kyrkhultsstugan.

"…The doors of the kitchen cupboard were painted in a magical blue which seemed to become darker on the inside. I can find no word to describe this colour. I have never encountered it since…"

Marie Hermanson, in: *Musselstranden*

«…Les portes des placards, dans la cuisine, étaient peintes d'un bleu merveilleux, qui semblait s'approfondir vers l'intérieur. Je ne connais pas de mot pour cette tonalité de bleu. Je n'ai jamais revu la même…»

Marie Hermanson, dans : *Musselstranden*

»…Die Schranktüren in der Küche waren in märchenhaftem Blau gestrichen, das gleichsam nach innen tiefer wurde. Ich habe kein Wort für diesen Farbton. Er ist mir nie wieder begegnet…«

Marie Hermanson, in: *Muschelstrand*

DETAILS

Détails Details

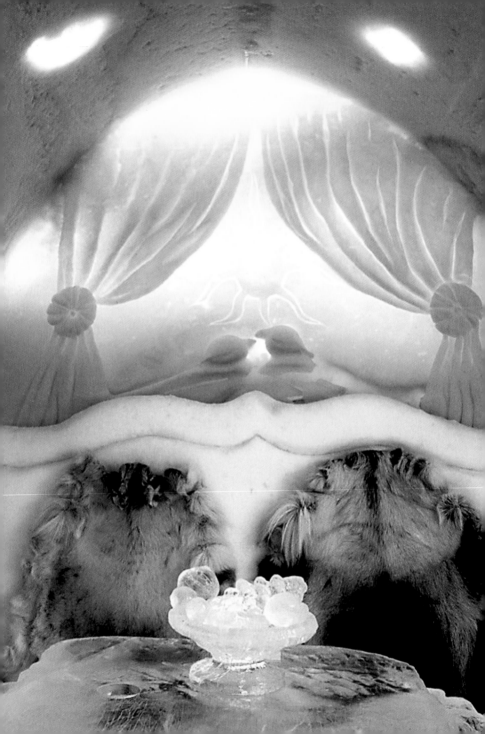

134 Togetherness: tea in front of a wooden house painted in typical Swedish red. *Vie à deux : l'heure du thé devant une maison en bois rouge suédois.* Zweisam: Teestunde vor einem Holzhaus in typisch schwedischem Rot.

136 Sweet and sour: freshly picked red currants. *Aigre-doux : groseilles fraîchement cueillies.* Süß-sauer: Frisch gepflückte Johannisbeeren.

137 Hearty: Swedish specialities. *Savoureuses: spécialités suédoises.* Herzhaft: Schwedische Spezialitäten.

138 Fireplace: cooking on an old metal stove. *Le foyer : cuisiner sur un poêle ancien.* Feuerstelle: Kochen auf einem antiken Eisenherd.

140 Hand-carved: wooden toy horses. *Jouets sculptés main : chevaux de bois.* Handgeschnitzt: Spielzeugpferde aus Holz.

141 Cut and dried: sunflower blossom. *Séchée : une fleur de tournesol.* Getrocknet: Die Blüte einer Sonnenblume

142 To and fro: hammock in a garden. *Se balancer : hamac dans le jardin.* Hin und her schaukeln: Hängematte im Garten. .

144 Enticing light: candles in a window. *Signes lumineux : trois bougies à la fenêtre.* Leuchtzeichen: Drei Kerzen im Fenster.

145 Mouth-watering: juicy water melon. *L'eau à la bouche : melon juteux.* Zum Reinbeißen: Saftige Wassermelone.

146 Strong colours: in Carl Larsson's living room, Dalarna. *Couleurs soutenues : dans le salon de Carl Larsson, Dalarna.* Kräftige Farben: Im Wohnzimmer von Carl Larsson, Dalarna.

148 Simply beautiful: white crockery at the window. *Simple et beau : vaisselle blanche à la fenêtre de la cuisine.* Schlicht und schön: Weißes Geschirr am Küchenfenster.

149 Fellow occupant: Martine Colliander's cat, Stockholm. *Colocataire : le chat de Martine Colliander, Stockholm.* Mitbewohnerin: Die Katze von Martine Colliander, Stockholm.

150 For twittering guests: a wooden starlings' house. *Petite maison de bois pour hôtes gazouillants : couveuse pour sansonnets.* Holzhäuschen für zwitschernde Gäste: Starenkästen.

152 Art in ice: at the Ice Hotel in Jukkasjärvi, northern Sweden. *Art figé : dans l'hôtel de glace de Jukkasjärvi, Suède du Nord.* Gefrorene Kunst: Im Icehotel in Jukkasjärvi, Nordschweden.

153 Translucent furniture: in the Ice Hotel in Jukkasjärvi, northern Sweden. *Meubles transparents : dans le l'hôtel de glace de Jukkasjärvi, Suède du Nord.* Durchsichtige Möbel: Im Icehotel in Jukkasjärvi, Nordschweden.

154 Ornate: chaise longue in the small castle in Haga, Uppland. *Richement décorée : la chaise-longue dans le petit château de Haga, Uppland.* Reich verziert: Chaiselongue im Schlösschen von Haga, Uppland.

156/157 Trompe-l'œil: in Leufsta Castle, Uppland (left) and the home of Carl von Linné (right). *Technique du trompe-l'œil : au château de Leufsta, Uppland (à gauche) et dans la maison de Carl von Linné (à droite).* Trompe-l'œil-Technik: Auf Schloss Leufsta, Uppland (links) und im Haus von Carl von Linné (rechts).

158 White and blue: coffee pot, dishes, and Delft tiles in Hans Malmborg's house. *Bleus et blancs : cafetière, bols et carreaux de Delft chez Hans Malmborg.* Weiß-blau: Kaffeekanne, Schalen und Delfter Kacheln bei Hans Malmborg.

160 Gustavian style: chair in Svartsjö Castle, Mälaren. *Dans le style gustavien : chaise au château de Svartsjö, Mälaren.* Im gustavianischen Stil: Stuhl auf Schloss Svartsjö, Mälaren.

161 La grande dame: portrait of Queen Lovisa Ulrike in Svartsjö Castle. *Grande Dame : un portrait de la reine Lovisa Ulrike au château de Svartsjö.* Grande Dame: Ein Porträt von Königin Lovisa Ulrike auf Schloss Svartsjö.

162 Aromatic camomile: in Groddagården House on Gotland. *Le parfum de la camomille : dans la maison Groddagården sur l'île de Gotland.* Der Duft von Kamille: Im Haus Groddagården auf Gotland.

164 Glass decoration: five-armed candlestick. *Bijou en verre : candélabre à cinq branches.* Schmuckstück aus Glas: Fünfarmiger Kerzenleuchter.

165 Breakfast at Tiffany's: and at Martine Colliander's, Stockholm. *Petit déjeuner chez Tiffany : et chez Martine Colliander, Stockholm.* Frühstück bei Tiffany: Und bei Martine Colliander, Stockholm.

166 Apple harvest: in Varpet House, southeast of Stockholm. *Récolte de pommes : dans la maison Varpet, au sud-est de Stockholm.* Apfelernte: Im Haus Varpet, südöstlich von Stockholm.

168/169 Predominantly white: Martine Colliander's home, Stockholm. *Rêves d'intérieurs en blanc : chez Martine Colliander, Stockholm.* Wohnträume in Weiß: Bei Martine Colliander, Stockholm.

170 Fruity: jam and
fresh fruit in Varpet.
*Fruité : gelée et fruits
frais dans la maison
Varpet.* Fruchtig:
Gelee und frisches
Obst in Varpet.

172 Aromatic herbs:
in front of Hans Malm-
borg's door, Skåne.
*Herbes aromatiques :
devant la porte de
Hans Malmborg,
Skåne.* Aromatische
Kräuter: Vor der
Haustür von Hans
Malmborg, Skåne.

173 Neat and clean:
the only bathroom in
the country residence
of Löftstad. *Propre-
té : la seule salle de
bain dans le château
de plaisance de Löft-
stad.* Saubere
Sache: Das einzige
Badezimmer im Land-
schloss von Löftstad.

174 Layered: wood
in front of the house
of Carl von Linné,
Uppland. *Coupé en
rondins: du bois
devant la maison de
Carl von Linné, Upp-
land.* In Scheiben
geschnitten: Holz vor
dem Haus von Carl
von Linné, Uppland.

176 Blossoms:
colourful details in
Martine Colliander's
house, Stockholm.
*Floraison : détails
multicolores chez
Martine Colliander,
Stockholm.* Blütezeit:
Bunte Details bei
Martine Colliander,
Stockholm.

177 Vitamins: bowl
of fruit in Varpet,
southeast of Stock-
holm. *Vitamines :
coupe de fruits chez
Varpet, au sud-est de
Stockholm.* Vita-
mine: Obstschale in
Varpet, südöstlich
von Stockholm.

178 Still-life: at
Johan Brauner's on
Gotland. *Nature
morte : chez Johan
Brauner sur l'île de
Gotland.* Stillleben:
Bei Johan Brauner
auf Gotland.

180 In the light:
plants in Hans Malm-
borg's house, Skåne.
*Tournée vers la
lumière : plante dans
la maison de Hans
Malmborg, Skåne.*
Dem Licht zuge-
wandt: Pflanze im
Haus von Hans
Malmborg, Skåne.

181 Up to dry: in
Astrid Lindgren's
kitchen in Näs, Små-
land. *Linge à sécher :
dans la cuisine
d'Astrid Lindgren à
Näs, Småland.* Zum
Trocknen aufge-
hängt: In der Küche
von Astrid Lindgren
in Näs, Småland.

182 Karin's portrait:
on the door to Carl
Larsson's studio,
Dalarna. *Le portrait
de Karine : sur la
porte d'entrée de
l'atelier de Carl Lars-
son, Dalarna.* Karins
Porträt: An der Ein-
gangstür zum Atelier
von Carl Larsson,
Dalarna.

184 Of primary
importance: Albert
Engström's paint-box,
Uppland. *L'ustensile
le plus important : la
boîte à couleurs
d'Albert Engström,
Uppland.* Das
wichtigste Utensil: Der
Farbkasten von Albert
Engström, Uppland.

185 Past times: tools
and easel belonging
to Albert Engström.
*Témoins du passé :
outils et chevalet
d'Albert Engström.*
Zeugen der Vergan-
genheit: Werkzeug
und eine Staffelei von
Albert Engström.

186 Then as now:
rainwater barrel in
Varpet, southeast of
Stockholm. *Hier
comme aujourd'hui :
le réservoir d'eau de
pluie de Varpet, au
sud-est de Stockholm.*
Damals wie heute:
Die Regentonne von
Varpet, südöstlich
von Stockholm.

Photo Credits

**FRONT COVER /
COUVERTURE /
UMSCHLAGVORDERSEITE**
© Mads Mogensen

**BACK COVER /
DOS DE COUVERTURE /
UMSCHLAGRÜCKSEITE**
© René Stoeltie

10/11
© Jan Jordan

12/13
© René Stoeltie

14/15
© René Stoeltie

16/17
© René Stoeltie

18/19
© Mad Mogensen

20/21
© René Stoeltie

22/23
© René Stoeltie

24/25
© René Stoeltie

26/27
© René Stoeltie

28/29
© René Stoeltie

30/31
© René Stoeltie

32/33
© René Stoeltie

34/35
© René Stoeltie

36/37
© René Stoeltie

38/39
© René Stoeltie

40/41
© René Stoeltie

42/43
© Ingalill Snitt/ Inside

44/45
© René Stoeltie

46/47
© René Stoeltie

48/49
© Ingalill Snitt

54/55
© Jan Jordan

56/57
© Jan Jordan

58/59
© Mad Mogensen

60/61
© Mad Mogensen

62/63
© René Stoeltie

64/65
© René Stoeltie

66/67
© René Stoeltie

68/69
© René Stoeltie

70/71
© René Stoeltie

72/73
© René Stoeltie

74/75
© René Stoeltie

76/77
© René Stoeltie

78/79
© René Stoeltie

80/81
© René Stoeltie

82/83
© Ingalill Snitt

84/85
© René Stoeltie

86/87
© René Stoeltie

88/89
© Ingalill Snitt

90/91
© René Stoeltie

92/93
© René Stoeltie

94/95
© René Stoeltie

96/97
© René Stoeltie

98/99
© René Stoeltie

100/101
© René Stoeltie

102/103
© René Stoeltie

104/105
© René Stoeltie

106/107
© René Stoeltie

108/109
© René Stoeltie

110/111
© René Stoeltie

112/113
© René Stoeltie

114/115
© René Stoeltie

116/117
© Ingalill Snitt/ Inside

118/119
© René Stoeltie

120/121
© Ingalill Snitt/ Inside

122/123
© Ingalill Snitt/ Inside

124/125
© René Stoeltie

126/127
© René Stoeltie

134
© Mad Mogensen

136
© Mad Mogensen

137
© Mad Mogensen

138
© Mad Mogensen

140
© Mad Mogensen

141
© Mad Mogensen

142
© Mad Mogensen

144
© Mad Mogensen

145
© Mad Mogensen

146
© René Stoeltie

148
© Mad Mogensen

149
© René Stoeltie

150
© Mad Mogensen

152
© Jan Jordan

153
© Jan Jordan

154
© René Stoeltie

156/157
© René Stoeltie

158
© René Stoeltie

160
© René Stoeltie

161
© René Stoeltie

162
© Ingalill Snitt

164
© René Stoeltie

165
© René Stoeltie

166
© René Stoeltie

168/169
© René Stoeltie

170
© René Stoeltie

172
© René Stoeltie

173
© René Stoeltie

174
© René Stoeltie

176
© René Stoeltie

177
© René Stoeltie

178
© Ingalill Snitt/ Inside

180
© René Stoeltie

181
© René Stoeltie

182
© René Stoeltie

184
© René Stoeltie

185
© René Stoeltie

186
© René Stoeltie

The Hotel Book. Great Escapes South America Christiane Reiter / Ed. Angelika Taschen / Hardcover, 360 pp. / € 29.99 / $ 39.99 / £ 24.99 / ¥ 5.900

The Hotel Book. Great Escapes North America Daisann McLane / Ed. Angelika Taschen / Hardcover, 400 pp. / € 29.99 / $ 39.99 / £ 24.99 / ¥ 5.900

The Hotel Book. Great Escapes Asia Christiane Reiter / Ed. Angelika Taschen / Hardcover, 400 pp. / € 29.99 / $ 39.99 / £ 24.99 / ¥ 5.900

"This is one for the coffee table, providing more than enough material for a good drool. Gorgeousness between the cover." —*Time Out*, London, on *Great Escapes Africa*

"Buy them all and add some pleasure to your life."

60s Fashion
Ed. Jim Heimann

70s Fashion
Ed. Jim Heimann

African Style
Ed. Angelika Taschen

Alchemy & Mysticism
Alexander Roob

American Indian
Dr. Sonja Schierle

Angels
Gilles Néret

Architecture Now!
Ed. Philip Jodidio

Art Now
Eds. Burkhard Riemschneider,
Uta Grosenick

Atget's Paris
Ed. Hans Christian Adam

Bamboo Style
Ed. Angelika Taschen

Ingrid Bergman
Ed. Paul Duncan, Scott Eyman

Berlin Style
Ed. Angelika Taschen

Humphrey Bogart
Ed. Paul Duncan, James Ursini

Marlon Brando
Ed. Paul Duncan,
F.X. Feeney

Brussels Style
Ed. Angelika Taschen

Cars of the 50s
Ed. Jim Heimann,
Tony Thacker

Cars of the 60s
Ed. Jim Heimann, Tony Thacker

Cars of the 70s
Ed. Jim Heimann, Tony Thacker

Charlie Chaplin
Ed. Paul Duncan, David Robinson

China Style
Ed. Angelika Taschen

Christmas
Ed. Jim Heimann, Steven Heller

Design Handbook
Charlotte & Peter Fiell

Design for the 21st Century
Eds. Charlotte & Peter Fiell

Design of the 20th Century
Eds. Charlotte & Peter Fiell

Marlene Dietrich
Ed. Paul Duncan,
James Ursini

Devils
Gilles Néret

Robert Doisneau
Ed. Jean-Claude Gautrand

East German Design
Ralf Ulrich/Photos: Ernst Hedler

Clint Eastwood
Ed. Paul Duncan, Douglas
Keesey

Egypt Style
Ed. Angelika Taschen

Encyclopaedia Anatomica
Ed. Museo La Specola Florence

M.C. Escher

Fashion
Ed. The Kyoto Costume Institute

Fashion Now!
Eds. Terry Jones, Susie Rushton

Fruit
Ed. George Brookshaw,
Uta Pellgrü-Gagel

HR Giger
HR Giger

Grand Tour
Harry Seidler

Cary Grant
Ed. Paul Duncan, F.X. Feeney

Graphic Design
Eds. Charlotte & Peter Fiell

Greece Style
Ed. Angelika Taschen

Halloween
Ed. Jim Heimann,
Steven Heller

Havana Style
Ed. Angelika Taschen

Audrey Hepburn
Ed. Paul Duncan, F.X. Feeney

Katharine Hepburn
Ed. Paul Duncan, Alain Silver

Homo Art
Gilles Néret

Hot Rods
Ed. Coco Shinomiya, Tony
Thacker

Hula
Ed. Jim Heimann

India Bazaar
Samantha Harrison, Bari Kumar

London Style
Ed. Angelika Taschen

Steve McQueen
Ed. Paul Duncan, Alain Silver

Mexico Style
Ed. Angelika Taschen

Miami Style
Ed. Angelika Taschen

Minimal Style
Ed. Angelika Taschen

Marilyn Monroe
Ed. Paul Duncan,
F.X. Feeney

Morocco Style
Ed. Angelika Taschen

New York Style
Ed. Angelika Taschen

Paris Style
Ed. Angelika Taschen

Penguin
Frans Lanting

20th Century Photography
Museum Ludwig Cologne

Pierre et Gilles
Eric Troncy

Provence Style
Ed. Angelika Taschen

Robots & Spaceships
Ed. Teruhisa Kitahara

Safari Style
Ed. Angelika Taschen

Seaside Style
Ed. Angelika Taschen

Signs
Ed. Julius Wiedeman

South African Style
Ed. Angelika Taschen

Starck
Philippe Starck

Surfing
Ed. Jim Heimann

Sweden Style
Ed. Angelika Taschen

Tattoos
Ed. Henk Schiffmacher

Tiffany
Jacob Baal-Teshuva

Tokyo Style
Ed. Angelika Taschen

Tuscany Style
Ed. Angelika Taschen

Valentines
Ed. Jim Heimann,
Steven Heller

Web Design: Best Studios
Ed. Julius Wiedemann

Web Design: Best Studios 2
Ed. Julius Wiedemann

Web Design: E-Commerce
Ed. Julius Wiedemann

Web Design: Flash Sites
Ed. Julius Wiedemann

Web Design: Music Sites
Ed. Julius Wiedemann

Web Design: Portfolios
Ed. Julius Wiedemann

Orson Welles
Ed. Paul Duncan,
F.X. Feeney

Women Artists
in the 20th and 21st Century
Ed. Uta Grosenick

ICONS